HOLMESPUN

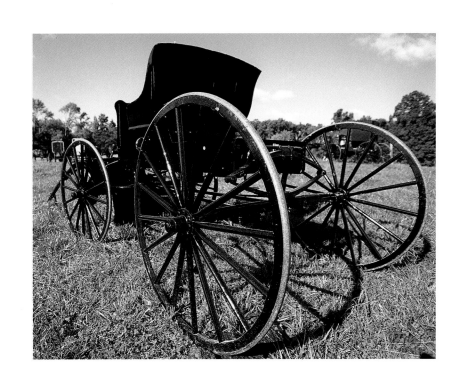

H·O·L·M·E·S·P·U·N

An Intimate Portrait of an Amish and Mennonite Community

PHOTOGRAPHS BY

Amanda Lumry & Loren Wengerd

TEXT BY

Laura Hurwitz

EaglemonT
Press

All photographs taken by Amanda Lumry and Loren Wengerd except:
pg. 25 sunset by Rufus Lumry
pg. 15 schoolhouse, pg. 47 mailbox, pg. 50 birdhouses, pg. 103 farmer and pg. 126 fence by Worth Lumry
pg. 99 farmers and endpaper by Chris Lumry

Illustrations by Julie Ruth

Book and cover design by Michael E. Penman

Digital imaging by Wy'east Color Inc. Bellevue, Washington

Printed in China by C&C Offset printing Co., Ltd.

Library of Congress Control Number: 2002103940

ISBN 0-9662257-6-7

10   9   8   7   6   5   4   3   2

First Edition Published by Eaglemont Press
PMB 741
15600 NE 8th #B-1
Bellevue, WA 98008
(425) 462-6618
info@eaglemontpress.com
www.eaglemontpress.com

A portion of the proceeds from this book are donated to the Mennonite Information Center
in Holmes County Ohio. For more information about this organization, please contact:

Mennonite Information Center
5798 County Road (CR) 77
P.O. Box 324
Berlin, OH 44610
phone: 330-893-3192
e-mail: behalt@sssnet.com

DEDICATION

This book is dedicated to the people of Holmes County - past, present, and future generations.

This is a community set apart, dedicated to God. Their strong Christian faith frames every aspect of their lives, family values and work ethic. These commonalities bind Holmes County residents together, and the result is a spiritual radiance which echoes the physical beauty of the rural, rolling terrain. This profound quality has nothing to do with vanity or pride and everything to do with God's works, both outer and inner.

It is to these truly beautiful people, many of whom have opened their homes and hearts to us, that we dedicate this book.

We would also like to make a special mention of Coach Perry Reese (the basketball coach for Hiland High School), who came to Holmes County a stranger and passed on as a beloved brother. His life of selflessness and forgiveness of people's insensitivities left an indelible mark on all of us who knew him well.

We love you, Coach.

Table of Co

ntents

Foreword ◆ viii

Map ◆ x

Acknowledgements ◆ xi

Introduction ◆ xii

God's People ◆ 1

Keeping A Home ◆ 33

The Community ◆ 55

By Hand ◆ 97

Seasons ◆ 123

FOREWORD

My initial stroll through this book brought smiles to my face at almost every turn of the page. The scenes were familiar, warming, reassuring. I knew those places, those homes, those farms. I had driven those roads, walked those paths. I knew those fields, and many of the people pictured. It was like I was hundreds of miles away, and was brought home by the brilliant and creative photography of Loren and Amanda.

Like Holmes County itself, what they have captured on film is just the way it is. For verification, all I have to do is look out my window, or step out onto the back porch and inhale that fresh spring air. Hopefully, my Amish neighbors haven't cleaned out the barn and spread the results onto their fertile fields.

Coupled with Laura's first-person narrative, the contents of this amazing book are like no other about Holmes County. That's because through their words and their pictures they have given an inside-out view of the world's largest Amish and Mennonite population. It is personal, precious, and true, all of it.

For Loren, especially, it was important to get it right. He was born and raised here, and in a way, this is as much his story as it is the Holmes County story. His reputation and that of his family, if you will, was on the line, and the story told here with words and pictures only enhances it. When you grow up in a locale and culture where the social, political, religious, and economic aspects of life are all intertwined, you had better carefully choose your words, and in this case, pictures, too. They have.

The work ethic, the family values, the commitment to community over self are all revealed in a marvelous and beautiful array of photography and text. This is a book which one will never tire of reading or leafing through. It is ageless and timely all in one marvelous volume.

– Bruce Stambaugh

Bruce Stambaugh is a newspaper columnist, a retired educator, and he serves as community relation's coordinator at Walnut Hills Retirement Community in Walnut Creek. He has lived all of his adult life with his wife, Neva, in Holmes County.

OHIO

90 Toledo
90
Cleveland
76
Akron
75
71 Canton
Holmes County
77
Great Miami River
70
Ohio River
Columbus
Dayton
Muskingum River
Cincinnati
Ohio River

ACKNOWLEDGEMENTS

We would like to thank the Lord for providing this wonderful opportunity to put together a book on the Amish and Mennonite community of Holmes County.

Thank you, Eli and Marcella Wengerd, for your constant support and invaluable advice.

We would like to thank Behalt! for its role in preserving the Amish and Mennonite culture, heritage and history.

We would like to thank Bruce Stambaugh for his dedication in preserving Amish and Mennonite heritage.

Rufus and Pat - another project we could not have done without your encouragement!

Sam and the kids, thank you for your love and patience.

Michael Penman, thank you for your design talent and the sense of excitement (and humor) that you have provided.

Thank you, Kim Henwood, for your organizational skills and boundless energy.

Nanda Mehta, Scott Drum, Joni Bomstead, Maryan Reagan and Greg Forge - thank you for your continued support of our endeavors.

We would like to thank J.R. Schrock for his impressive knowledge and numerous resources.

We would like to thank Eli Bauman for his unflagging enthusiasm and priceless counsel.

Thanks to Grant and the Wy'East team, and C&C Offset Printing Co., Ltd. for a job well done.

Julie Ruth, thank you for your gentle and inspired illustrations.

INTRODUCTION

It was a typical January day in northern Ohio, with a biting north wind and slate gray sky. After arriving at the Canton/Akron airport, we rented a car and drove past the strip malls with their familiar shops and restaurants. Starving, we stopped at a Taco Bell, wolfed down some burritos, and proceeded down the busy highway. *This could be Anywhere, USA,* I recall thinking. I simply couldn't imagine that we were nearing the largest Amish settlement in the country. All the ubiquitous trappings of modern life surrounded us.

We took the exit into the town of Sugarcreek and promptly found ourselves several steps back in both time and feeling. Sugarcreek is not flashy. It's comfortably worn and faded, with its cluster of charming older homes lining the narrow, hilly streets. We continued on down the road, following our map towards Mt. Hope. Our destination was the auction barn.

Mt. Hope is small, with no stop lights, gas stations or fast food restaurants. The auction building was large and unabashedly shabby. Parked outside on the frozen ridges of mud and ice were rows of cars and pick-up trucks and, along the side of the lot near the fence, lines of buggies. We found a parking spot and walked across the icy lot, through an

unheated hallway, and up the worn wooden steps to the seating arena. It was comparatively warm inside the auction barn, and very close. We sat on wooden platforms, which doubled as steps. The smells in the barn were difficult to isolate and identify - damp wool, hot dogs, and horse manure? We watched as scruffy ponies, enormous Clydesdales, elegant carriage horses, and horses one step away from the glue factory were paraded about, then shuttled back into the holding stalls while the calling and bidding proceeded at a breakneck pace.

I looked at the people around me. There were Amish, Mennonites, and some people who looked as secular as we did. A young Amish father, with one son on his lap, and another nestled by his side, captured my attention. He looked so doting, so earnestly protective. Clearly, love of family runs deep.

Perhaps it's more common to introduce a photographic book on Holmes County by describing the luxuriant rolling green hills dotted with simple white farmhouses, or the quaint buggies, or the cows grazing, or women in their bonnets and shawls. That is the postcard version of Amish country, the

image of that culture with which most of us are familiar. In fact, the physical beauty and charm of Holmes County is captured in the images of this book. However, there is a sort of beauty that is not so readily apparent, a deeper loveliness seen only by looking at both Amish and Mennonites. In a faded auction house in the small town of Mt. Hope on a frigid January afternoon, the true heart and soul of Holmes County made itself plain. There was nothing showy, nothing deliberate or geared to charm tourists. Everything in that barn spoke of functionality and common sense, coupled with an overwhelming sense of community and family values. While both preserve their distinct way of life, the Amish and Mennonite communities co-exist and support each other, and open their doors wide to everyone, friend, family, and stranger alike.

Initially, people here may identify themselves by their differences. "Stellet euch nicht dieser Welt gleich," ("Be ye not conformed to this world,") Romans 12:2, is the oft-cited biblical passage they use to define the reason for their simpler lives. However, the presence of love in the crook of a doting father's arm, of cooperative effort to reach common goals in the sing-song voice of the auctioneer, the capable handling of the horses and bids made by both the sellers and the auction house employees, and the inclusive community in the blend of people from different backgrounds sitting companionably together is what I saw at work in the auction barn that winter day, and for me this defines Holmes County, Ohio.

God's People

GOD'S PEOPLE

Religious History

Both the Amish and the Mennonites can trace their roots back to the Anabaptist movement, which started in 1525 in Zurich, Switzerland. These were the turbulent times of the Reformation, and Anabaptists felt very strongly about baptizing church members as adults upon an actual confession of faith rather than infants who were baptized without their consent, which was what the Catholics had mandated.

Knowing this departure from church law was considered heresy, and rather than drawing attention to themselves and risking expulsion or even death, Anabaptists led religious services secretly in their homes. Even though they kept a low profile, many were put to death or martyred during this time. The movement, however, not only survived this persecution, it flourished. Then, in 1536, a Catholic priest from Holland named Menno Simmons joined the Anabaptist movement. Because of his persistent and faithful leadership, this loosely organized group of Anabaptists eventually came to be known as Mennonites.

Previous Page: Want a ride on a buggy?
Opposite: A two horsepower buggy.

A way of life dating back to 1525...

Then, much later, in 1693, a bishop of the
church, Jacob Amman, broke away from the rest of the
Swiss Mennonites when they refused to enforce the practice
of shunning excommunicated members. He took other
members with him, and they became known as the
Amish Mennonites. In time, they were simply called the
Amish. Eventually, both groups took advantage of the
opportunity for freedom of religious expression in
America, and many Amish and Mennonites made the
long journey to the New World. Today, Amish communities
exist in twenty-four states. The largest of these is found
in Holmes County, Ohio.

Above: How many seasons has this sign seen?

Above: Walking together.

Above: A 1951 Mennonite tent meeting with Evangelist George R. Brunk, Jr.

Above: An Amish bench wagon provides easy storage and mobility for church and community gatherings.

Above: "Gott ist die Liebe."

There are many differences between Amish and Mennonites. Mennonites drive cars, use electricity, and attend school through high school and even college. The Amish do not own cars (but are allowed to ride with non-Amish drivers), do not have electricity in their homes, and for the most part attend only Amish schools that carry them through eighth grade. The Amish hold church services in members' homes and even, especially during the summer, their barns. Each family takes turns hosting church services throughout the year. This is a custom carried over from the early days in Europe, when they were forced to conduct their services in secret. Mennonites attend worship services in a church building.

Mennonites speak English both in public life and during worship services, but the Amish speak Pennsylvania Dutch amongst themselves and conduct their church services in the original Swiss German, using the hymnal and Bible sanctioned by the Swiss Brethren.

There are different sects of both Mennonites and Amish. For example, in Holmes County, one can find the Beachy Amish, who are the least conservative branch of Amish, the New Order Amish, who are more strict than the Beachy Amish, but less so than other groups (men are allowed to trim their beards, for example), the Old

Order Amish, who are more conservative in their interpretation of Amish law, and the Swartzentruber Amish, who are the most conservative (no indoor plumbing in their homes or even rubber treads on their wooden buggy wheels). The Mennonites, too, are divided into conservative and less conservative branches.

One interesting point is that the Amish and Mennonites amicably co-exist and support each other within their communities. In fact, not only do they get along together, the Amish and Mennonite communities don't even judge the outside world harshly. They quietly observe its flaws and steadfastly set themselves apart.

In the Amish community, adherence to strict codes of dress are important symbols of solidarity. For example, Amish men, once married, must wear a full beard. All Amish men wear dark clothing with suspenders, black or straw hats with a brim, and no outside or hip pockets on their trousers. Amish women must wear modest one-piece solid fabric dresses cut no shorter than eight inches from the floor.

Above: Two Amish men share a morning walk together.

They are not allowed to cut, adorn, or curl their hair, and aprons, shawls, and bonnets of proper size and color must be worn at appropriate times. These ordained styles of dress, the Amish feel, are an expression of their obedience to God and a form of rejection of the proud and ungodly modern world. There are even distinctions in dress within the Amish community which identify the wearer's age, sex, and role in society. To illustrate this point, the Kapp, or head cap worn by Amish females and even infants, is a black cap worn on Sundays and a white cap worn at home the rest of the week. This changes, after marriage, to a white cap which is worn at all times.

Mennonite men typically dress in conservative conventional clothing, and are often indistinguishable from men outside the community. However, for more formal occasions, conservative Mennonite men wear a "straight-cut" suit jacket, as opposed to a typical tailored suit with a lapel. This suit resembles a Bombay jacket. Mennonite women wear a wide range of clothing, from plain dress with a covering to dressing like the rest of mainstream society. It simply depends on which congregation and church conference they belong to. Conservative Mennonite women wear dresses, as modest in cut as those worn by Amish women, but they are allowed to use fabric with

Above: Kapp - an Amish woman's head covering.

bright colors and patterns. Like the Amish, they also do not cut their hair and they wear head coverings. These coverings are similar but slightly smaller than those worn by Amish women.

Both the Amish and the Mennonites are pacifists. It is part of their shared religious heritage to refuse to take up arms against other human beings. They quote the teachings of Jesus from the Bible, Matthew 5:44: "But I say unto you, Love your enemies, bless them that curse you, do good to them that hate you, and pray for those that despitefully use you and persecute you." They feel very strongly that evil should not be repaid with evil, and it is better to suffer wrong than to inflict it. During times of war, Amish and Mennonite men serve their country in some non-military alternative service. Some more traditional thinkers for whom any type of government service is unacceptable choose to serve time in jail instead.

The common theological and philosophical roots of both the Amish and the Mennonites can be seen in their similarities: their belief in baptizing adults, their literal interpretation of the Bible, their strict adherence to dress and behavioral rules and customs, and their refusal to bear arms against their fellow man.

Behalt!

A highly enlightening and educational trip one
can take when visiting Holmes County is to the
Mennonite Information Center near Berlin. There, one
can see the cyclorama "Behalt!" which depicts the history
of the Anabaptist movement. Heinz Gaugel, a German-
born self-taught artist, began this enormous (10 by 265
foot) mural in 1972. The mural spans the entire wall
surface of the cavernous, circular room which houses it,

and the viewer must move around
the room to see the entire history of
the Mennonite, Amish, and the
lesser-known but related Hutterites
(note: no Hutterite settlements exist
in Holmes County).

The often violent history of the
persecution of the Anabaptists by
the Catholic church is graphically
depicted, and it is fascinating to
hear the Mennonite docents explain
each illustration.

Sunday Dinner

Our own experience with a traditional Mennonite Sunday dinner brings back some of the warmest memories of our time in Holmes County.

Everyone attends church, which for us consisted of a brief worship and fellowship meeting in the sanctuary, then the parishioners divide into groups determined by gender and age. Everyone then leaves for separate classrooms to attend Sunday School for an hour or so. For example, there is a class for young married women, a class for older married women, and a class for women with grandchildren. Men, children and teens have their own classes.

These classes are intimate and headed by a lay member of the congregation. There is a scripture lesson for the day, and everyone is encouraged to join in with their interpretation of the Biblical passage or story selected. The atmosphere in class was casual and encouraging, and no viewpoint is ever dismissed. There is a great deal of laughter as well as free-flowing debate. A bell sounds to indicate that it is time to go upstairs and re-congregate for the rest of the morning's service.

After several songs, some church news, and the sermon itself, church is over for the morning. (Often, there will be another service on Sunday night and one on Wednesday.) Congregants rise and gather in the foyer outside the sanctuary to greet one another and

Above: It's important to eat your daily bread - spiritually and physically!

Local Mennonite Churches

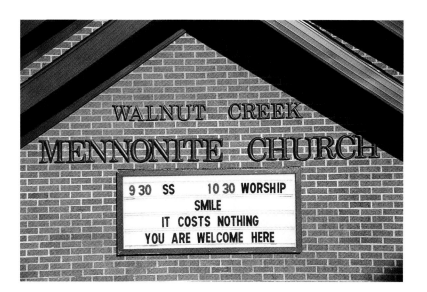

share news. It is an ideal time for connecting, and no one seems in any sort of rush to leave. After a time, though, we notice the crowd begin to thin out, so we get into the car and head back home.

Back at the house, the extra leaves are put in the table and chairs and high chairs are pulled up to accommodate the extended family. For us, this included four grandchildren, three sons and spouses, and the hosts. Food, which had been baking in the oven or was warmed up after we walked in the door, is promptly placed on the table. It is a true feast of baked chicken with dressing, noodles, potatoes, coleslaw, Jello salad, creamed cucumbers, baby corn, baked beans, applesauce and bread. After saying a prayer, we all eat until we are stuffed. The babies are fed, children eat heartily, and we all engage in spirited talk of both the good things and the bad things that have gone on during the week and also the plans for the week ahead. Then, the women get up to clear the dishes and put out the peach cobbler and ice cream for dessert.

Amazingly, considering the vast quantity of dinner we have consumed, we all swiftly polish off desert, then the women began to clean up in earnest while the men wander into the living room with the children to relax, play, and talk amongst themselves.

Left: Amish men waiting for the meeting to begin.

Clean up, with "many hands making light work" doesn't take long at all, and soon the women join the men. After a while, a game of "Take One," a variation on Scrabble, ensues, and all who want to play join in enthusiastically. Our hostess proves herself to be unbeatable. Cards is next on the game agenda, and a lively game called Dutch Blitz, which is an Amish card game requiring a fast brain and even faster hands, springs up. The children play with their toys, some of the less energetic adults snooze in their chairs, then, around six o'clock, rolls, cold cuts, cheese, ice cream, and popcorn are served for a light meal and after some more talk the extended family members gather up kids, coats, and dishes and depart for their respective homes.

Sunday dinner in most Holmes County households is an afternoon-long affair, and the dinner itself is only a part of it. It offers a chance to talk, laugh, play, and simply be together as a family, and to cherish the strength and security that closeness provides.

Above: Swings and see-saws wait expectantly for the Amish children to come out and play.

Clarence and Lois Miller

When we went to call on Clarence and Lois Miller, we were struck by the care they have taken with their furnishings, food, and decorative efforts. Before us was a delicious tea party spread, and the table was set with lovely china. Their furniture was Victorian era, and the room was full of items collected over the years, displayed in a beautiful way. Lois loves theme decorating, devoting a portion of wall and floor space to each theme. We were treated to her strawberry collection, complete with strawberry mugs and towels, and even a toy truck with a design from a feed mill in Pennsylvania!

Clarence and Lois Miller are a very calm, spiritual couple, united not only in marriage but in their faith. (We found this "oneness of faith" to be a common thread in marriages in this community).

Lois grew up in Kentucky, one of six children. Her parents had established a mission church, and they were the only Mennonites in the area. Lois went through the requisite training to become a nurse, finally moving up to Red Lake, Ontario, to serve as the nurse for a mission organization that ministers to Indians. She lived there for one year, finally moving to Holmes County after the death of her boyfriend.

Clarence was born and raised in Holmes County, also one of six children. His parents left the Amish faith after disagreeing with a Church policy, and they began a Beachy Amish (less conservative) church in Berlin. In 1975, Clarence's mother died, leaving his father to raise the family on his own.

Clarence and Lois have three children. Their eldest, Nicole, is in her twenties, and their two youngest, twins Matthew and Morgan, are almost twenty. Lois is a full time mother at this point, but has kept her nursing license current. She sees this as a practical necessity in a volatile economy. Clarence began his working life in construction. Now he is employed as an estimator for both commercial and residential structures at Holmes Lumber Building Center, and has worked there for the past fifteen years. He also serves as a deacon at the Sharon Mennonite Church. Holmes Lumber has been very flexible regarding his work hours, and this has enabled him to take time off to visit his parishioners as needed.

Both Clarence and Lois had some opinions about living in Holmes County. A common misconception? That the Amish are peaceful people. They do live quiet lives, but inside, they are just like any other human beings. They also point out the different branches of the faith: Beachy Amish, Conservative Mennonite, Old and New Order Amish, Swartzentruber Amish. The theology for all is much

the same, varying primarily in principles and practices. In other

words, the fundamentals are identical, but the understanding and

interpretation of those beliefs differ. Lois and Clarence both feel very

strongly about their faith and don't shy away from educating others.

Lois says, "We can be missionaries here in Holmes County to the

tourists." Clarence agrees. "The Behalt! Mural and Mennonite

Information Center provides a positive witness for tourists." Actually,

he finds the Center a useful teaching tool for his baptismal class

from his own congregation. (To find out more about Behalt!, see

page 9 of this chapter).

Tourism, as a rule, has been basically positive for the community.

Both think that tourism has provided a necessary means for Amish

Above: Tea time.

men to support their typically large families. The woodworking and hospitality related jobs bring in additional income.

Lois appreciates the lessons of her youth. She "values the importance of Scripture as truth." Clarence nods and says, for adult role models, "the walk and the talk should measure up." Have they passed these lessons onto their children? Most definitely. They also have taught their children the wisdom of saving money. They have a very sensible formula: 10% tithe, 10% family, 10% savings, 10% personal, 10% giving, 50% car fund.

Clearly, the focus for Clarence and Lois is on their faith, children, and community. With this in mind, they work hard, remain faithful, and teach by example. "The walk and the talk" without question, measure up. ✦

Left: The pulpit at Sharon Mennonite Church where Clarence delivers his inspired sermons.

LaVon and Kara Schrock

LaVon and Kara Shrock are a young Mennonite couple living in Sugarcreek. They have three children, six-year-old Claudia (well-behaved, organized, very artistic), three-year-old Miles (had some health problems as an infant but is now doing well, a bit reserved, thoughtful), and two-year-old Vaughn (the attention grabber, full of energy). LaVon hangs gutters and spouting for a living, and Kara is a full-time mother. They are intensely family-oriented. It was very clear from spending time with them that their faith and their children are the center of their world.

Left to Right: Claudia, Kara, LaVon, Miles and Vaughn.

LaVon grew up in South Carolina, one of twelve children (nine girls, three boys). He's the third youngest. LaVon values his heritage. He wants to pass on to his children the "lessons of responsibility, honesty, good morals, and hard work ethic." He does believe the parents, through deeds as well as through teaching, pass down these lessons. He likes the work he does, even though it is not easy. His favorite season is fall, because "it's good weather to work in, it's beautiful with the leaves changing color, and it's great when things start to slow down."

He seems to be a man committed to his young family and full of the desire to raise his children with good values and an emphasis on spiritual growth. He actually credits Kara with charging him with a renewed interest in Jesus. It seems when Kara began home schooling Claudia, she felt she could not teach her daughter about Jesus without it first being true to her, and her "hunger to press into Jesus" inspired LaVon.

Kara, like LaVon, is committed first to Christ and her family. She grew up as a Mennonite in Holmes County, and was one of three daughters. She loves having her children around and had a great deal to say about parenting: "Seems like each new childhood phase has new challenges. Finish one stage and you are right in another one," she observed ruefully. "But," she smiled, "the Lord does miracles when you have kids, especially when you have boys." Kara doesn't particularly like to cook. She likes trying to make food look attractive, but when it comes to everyday cooking, it just doesn't interest her much. She does, however, like to bake.

Kara's faith is her source of strength. She appreciates the Anabaptist founders of the Mennonite and Amish religion who were martyrs because of their faith. She does find it odd, however, that people put the Amish "on a pedestal." Their way of life doesn't make them more godly than anyone else. "They are born with the same nature as any other people." Kara also thinks that raising children in

Holmes County has its pros and cons. On one hand, it is a safe community, but on the other, "many things are done in the name of Christianity that are not really Christ-like."

Sitting around their kitchen table, eating ladyfinger popcorn and apple crisp and drinking coffee, it is clear to see that LaVon and Kara live for their little family. Whenever Claudia, Miles, or Vaughn need a lap or a kiss or a tickle, LaVon and Kara are there to provide it. They are also there to provide guidance, wisdom, and unconditional love.

Right: Harvest time.

Above: Some Amish still use subterranean spring houses to cool their perishables during the hot summer months. Items are placed in the left storage area where cold spring water flows.

Left: Don't forget to wash your hands!

Left: Since telephones are not allowed, this Amish man conducts business from the pay phone.

Right: The open-air hack buggy.

*"This is the first and greatest commandment:
Love the Lord God with all of your
heart and with all your soul and with
all your mind. And the second is like it:
Love your neighbor as yourself."*

- Matthew 22:37-39

Above: A Gig Saddle on a horse harness.

Right: A popular route through Holmes County.

Above: The key ignition in an Amish buggy is used to activate the battery operated signal lights.

Right: Caution: Slow moving vehicle!

Keeping A Home

KEEPING A HOME

Keeping a home, especially for those who choose to live without the aid of modern conveniences, requires energy, patience, and organization. This rather daunting task traditionally falls to women. In fact, there is a schedule to the prescribed weekly ordering of chores. This very systematic schedule has been passed down from mother to daughter for generations in Holmes County.

Monday - *Wash Day*

Tuesday - *Ironing Day*

Wednesday - *Mending Day*

Thursday - *Shopping Day*

Friday - *Cleaning Day*

Saturday - *Cooking Day*

Sunday - *The Lord's Day*

Previous Page: A late fall sunset casts a peaceful glow on this typical Amish home.
Opposite: Two Mennonite women diligently remove corn from the ears as they prepare for the next year.

It must be Saturday!

Above: Cutting up apples for applesauce.

Below: Washing clothes takes longer with the hand operated Maytag for this Amish family.

It's true, if you take a drive around Holmes County on a Monday, the clotheslines are full. I'm willing to wager that if you went visiting on a Tuesday, the ironing board and iron (heated on the stove) would be out in most Amish kitchens. Careful organization and the passing down of methods and traditions are a way of domestic life in each Amish household, and a standard Amish home (often containing many children) relies on order and a sense of established tradition to flow smoothly.

The many Amish homes we visited were amazingly calm and uncluttered. To enter a house and hear the silence that comes from the absence of electrical devices is almost eerie. There is no hum of a refrigerator or buzz of electric lights, no cacophony from a television or stereo or computer. There are no stacks of newspapers (maybe a modest copy of *The Budget*), no shelves full of paperback books (perhaps a spare assortment of religious books and a Bible). No family portraits line the walls, just an occasional painting of a landscape, or perhaps, a calendar.

As time-consuming as it must be to do the smallest chore without technology, there is a simplicity to Amish life that allows the focus to stay on the task at hand. This simplicity extends to the Mennonite lifestyle as well. While the Mennonites are able to use technology, their philosophy of family and faith are very similar to that of the Amish. As with the Amish, the children's activities are those of the entire family, with the exception of school. There isn't a car pool rushing off to sports practices and dance classes. The emphasis in both the Mennonite and Amish homes is on God and family. Certainly, people have hobbies and recreational activities, but home life does not revolve around those activities.

There is a strict distribution of labor in the majority of Amish homes. Women care for the children, cook, clean, quilt, make clothes for the children, and garden. Men do the heavy farm work, carpentry, meat curing, and work outside the home. This method of running a home holds true in most Conservative Mennonite homes as well. Generally speaking, while building and supporting the household is the work of men, the task of keeping a home falls to the women.

Above: A quilt brightens an otherwise Spartan Amish bedroom.

Below: An elegant Mennonite sitting room. Time to curl up and read a good book.

Above: ABC and number charts grace the wall of this old Amish home.

Above Right: This oil lamp is the single source of light for an Amish family's living room.

Right: Warm coats and a gas lantern for the morning chores.

Previous Page: Supper time approaches for this Mennonite family.

Above: Amish clothes drying on the line.

"…they can train the young women to love their husbands and children, to be self-controlled and pure, to be busy at home, to be kind, and to be subject to their husbands, so that no one will malign the word of God."

- Titus 2:4-5

Above: Beautiful peach rose in full bloom.

Right: This milk can gets a new lease on life.

Above: A typical morning fog wraps flowers in a soft blanket.

The Covering

"Now I want you to realize that the head of every man is Christ, and the head of the woman is man, and the head of Christ is God. Every man who prays or prophesies with his head covered dishonors his head. And every woman who prays or prophesies with her head uncovered dishonors her head–it is just as though her head were shaved. If a woman does not cover her head, she should have her hair cut off; and if it is a disgrace for a woman to have her hair cut off, she should cover her head. A man ought not to cover his head, since he is the image and glory of God; but the woman is the glory of man. For man did not come from woman, but woman from man; neither was man created for woman, but woman for man. For this reason, and because of the angels, the woman ought to have a sign of authority on her head."

- 1 Corinthians 11:3-10

Eli and Marcella Wengerd

Above: Eli and Marcella arrive home from church.

Eli and Marcella Wengerd have been married for thirty-eight years, and have raised five sons and a daughter, in addition to running several successful businesses, some sequential, some simultaneously. Among others, Eli has owned a grocery store and a gift store, a furniture store, a shoe store, and an exotic animal petting zoo featuring llamas, white-tail deer, peacocks, and other unusual creatures. He is a skilled licensed barber, merchant, and dog breeder– he currently raises Chihuahuas. Marcella joined Eli in several business ventures along the way, and together they now manage their thriving fabric and gift shop in Mt. Hope. They live in a spacious new home with a magnificent view of the rolling hills and valleys of rural Holmes County.

Visiting with these conservative Mennonites is an almost indescribably warm experience. Immediately one senses their connection and devotion to each other. Get to know them, and one sees how that connection and devotion extends to their family, to their church, and to the community at large.

Marcella grew up, the third oldest of seven children, in Kidron, Ohio. Her family belonged to the Swiss Mennonite church. It wasn't until she was fourteen that her family had an indoor toilet, but her memories are not inspired by their of lack of

Above: Eli reassures his granddaughter that the ouchie will be okay.

Eli was one of five children, the only boy, growing up in Wayne County, Ohio. His family was Amish until he was in second grade, when they became Mennonite. He remembers sleeping alone in his own room, listening as best he could to his sisters in the next room chat before they drifted off to sleep. Hating to be left out of the fun and longing to hear their bedtime conversation more clearly, eight-year-old Eli decided to punch a hole "the size of a cantaloupe" in the wall which separated the two rooms. "I thought it didn't matter too much, since my parents were only renting the house." He found out it did indeed matter, and the hole was patched. Eli maintains his closeness to his sisters. He talks to them and still teases them quite often.

Marcella's style is natural, simple, and dignified. She is slender and intelligent looking, with an air of competent calm. Organization

creature comforts. Instead, she recalls working hard in the garden with her sisters and brothers, then choosing one sibling to rush inside to make popcorn while the others cleaned up. Then, they would gather outside around the bowl of warm, freshly popped corn to see who could spot the first star in the evening sky.

is one of her many strong points, but she is warm and welcoming, never rushed. Marcella manages to get an amazing amount of things done without ever seeming hasty or hurried. An example: we were invited for supper at her home, and after she'd put in a full day of work at the shop, we watched in awe as she whipped everything together in what seemed to be three seconds flat. There were sloppy joe sandwiches, green beans, applesauce, fresh salad, corn, and peach cobbler - all of it delicious and homemade. We almost felt as if we were in the presence of a culinary magician. Then, after we ate, she orchestrated a kitchen clean up that also seemed to be completed in the blink of an eye, after which she sat down for some unhurried conversation.

Eli is broad-shouldered, handsome, and quick to grin. He makes everyone feel immediately at ease. Here is a man who loves his life. He has a wonderful voice, which he gets to test out weekly in his church's Men's Chorus practice. His dogs are his babies. In fact, I made the comment to him that if I believed in reincarnation, I would want to come back as one of his Chihuahuas. Initially, when Eli asked if we wanted to see the kennel, I imagined something very Spartan. Instead, from the outside, the kennel looks like a charming guest cottage, and inside, it is heated and pristine. Eli visits the dogs twice a day, to feed, clean up, chat, and play with them. When he enters the kennel, the canine equivalent of shouts of

joy start up, and every tail is wagging. Dogs know real love when they see it, and they see it in Eli.

While Eli's dogs are his babies, the real love of his life is Marcella. They met when they were ten and eleven years old, and started dating when they were in their late teens. Their sons, Phil, Marlin, Myron, and twins Loren and Doran, and their daughter, Sheri, are precious to them. They remain connected, even though life has presented new opportunities and several of the Wengerd children have moved away. Pictures of their children's weddings and their ever-growing crop of grandchildren line the walls, underscoring their parental devotion to their family. After supper, Eli and Marcella sit down in their comfortable living room and talk or read. They have no television set. They enjoy listening to Christian music on the radio, and Christian living radio shows, and they also listen to quite a few Cleveland Indians baseball games during the summer months.

Of course, life at the Wengerd's isn't all relaxation and quiet reflection. They are quite industrious: Marcella cans her own fruits and vegetables, helps sew quilts for her church which are sold at auction, and balances her store's books. Eli practices his music, works on various projects around the house, and is in charge of getting his dogs bred and sold as well as caring for them on a daily basis.

Inset: Amish coats and hats for sale at the fabric store.

Above: A typical trash burner for burnable items is permissible in the country.

Together, Eli and Marcella manage the Mt. Hope Fabrics and Gift Shoppe. Marcella runs the fabric business, while Eli takes care of ordering the hats and other clothing items, which are a large part of the trade they do with the Amish. Both Eli and Marcella enjoy traveling, most often to visit family.

Their church is the center of their social and spiritual life, and the Christian principles their parents instilled in them, which they in turn have passed down to their children, are heartfelt and unwavering.

Eli and Marcella are not only husband and wife, they are true partners, and their close union benefits many. Warmth, mutual respect and trust is all there for everyone to see. Their marriage is a sacred partnership and a solemn vow, but within that partnership there is room for laughter, independence, a loving family, a deep faith, and commitment to community. They are an inspiration.

Below: An Amish lady keeping up with the yard work.

Above: Black-eyed Susan flowers.

Above: It is popular to have bird houses for Purple Martins in one's yard.

Left: Three Amish girls head out for a ride with their pony. There are no driver's age limits here!

Right: Monday morning: clothes for the whole family hang on the line.

Left: Since creature comforts are not allowed in the home, these telephone booths dot the Amish landscape. Some are disguised and some obvious but each serves the same purpose – to connect people with each other and with the outside world.

Right: Horses and buggies wait to take home loads of groceries.

Canning and Preserving

In Amish and Mennonite homes, foods are preserved so that they can be enjoyed year round. Fruits, vegetables, and other perishable foods are used first when they are fresh, but any surpluses are carefully set aside so that they can be canned or preserved. Even meat is canned for use at a future date. This practice further demonstrates the Amish/Mennonite philosophy of thrift and complete dedication to wasting nothing.

Home canning takes time, but it is not complicated. Heat is applied to food placed in a sealed jar in order to kill off bacteria and microorganisms that would result in that particular food's spoilage. Fruits and vegetables are the most commonly preserved items, and they are processed at their peak of ripeness. In order to be preserved the foods are placed into canning jars with two-piece vacuum caps, then the filled jars are heated to a temperature high enough to kill all bacteria. Then, the jars are slowly cooled to allow them to seal. After they are cooled they may be dated and stored in a cool fruit cellar.

Amish and Mennonite women are skilled in the art of canning and preserving. It is another household task they perform which contributes to the health and economic welfare of their home.

Left: Provisions for the winter.

It seems that everywhere in Holmes County, there is an all-encompassing sense of community. A profound commitment to join together to work for the greater good starts at the most basic, personal level- the family unit- and carries through to their larger social groupings, those of church and neighborhood. This ultimately defines their world-view, which is one of benevolence, compassion, and charity.

Within the family, everyone works as a team to keep the household running smoothly. Even when children are quite young, they are assigned tasks and given a sense of the necessity and importance of their contribution. There is an emphasis on responsibility for the young and middle aged adults, while respect is afforded the elders, and a great deal of love and nurturing is heaped upon the young (that, and the occasional dose of discipline as needed). In the homes we visited, we saw no bickering children, no short-tempered parents with surly teenagers,

Previous Page: Amish youth gather for an afternoon of lively volleyball.
Opposite: Heading home with supplies.

"..benevolence, compassion and charity."

and no parent-child screaming matches. Instead, we watched as brothers and sisters played quietly and cooperatively, children obeyed parents without question, wives and husbands tacitly understood how best to help their spouse and simply did what needed to be done. The lack of tension and anxiety in these homes was truly quite remarkable.

Wholeheartedly and without hesitation, neighbors help neighbors. Whether taking up collections for families that have lost a breadwinner, or organizing to raise a barn, the community pulls together to take care of any need. This last example of working for the collective benefit is perhaps the defining example of community for the Amish and Mennonites of Holmes County.

Below: All that is left from the fire is the charred and blackened silo.

Barn Raisings

During the course of the work on this book, a barn, which had been built in 1868, was struck by lightning and burned to the ground on August 9, 2001. Firefighters from neighboring towns rushed to the blaze, but they were unable to save the structure. Within days, neighbors came out to help remove charred debris. A few days later, new footers and a new foundation were laid. At the same time, four loads of white oak logs donated and sawed by local lumber mills were hauled in to serve as beams and framing lumber. A date was set just a few weeks later to erect the new barn.

We arrived shortly after sunrise on the designated barn-raising day and watched in awe as close to a thousand Amish men and boys (two crews of 500) scrambled on high cross beams, and the staccato banging of hammers reverberated rhythmically. At noon, after the barn was essentially finished, the women served a huge meal to the workers. By early afternoon, the final runs of gutters and downspouts were hung and wagonloads of donated hay began to arrive. To see the completed barn was nothing short of miraculous.

"To think," I overheard an onlooker tell his wife, "this morning there was nothing there but a block wall foundation." It is amazing what many hands working together can accomplish!

Above: Diligent workers apply fascia.

Left: Time for a breather.

"Carry each other's burdens, and in this way you will fulfill the law of Christ." - **Galatians 6:2**

The work continues...

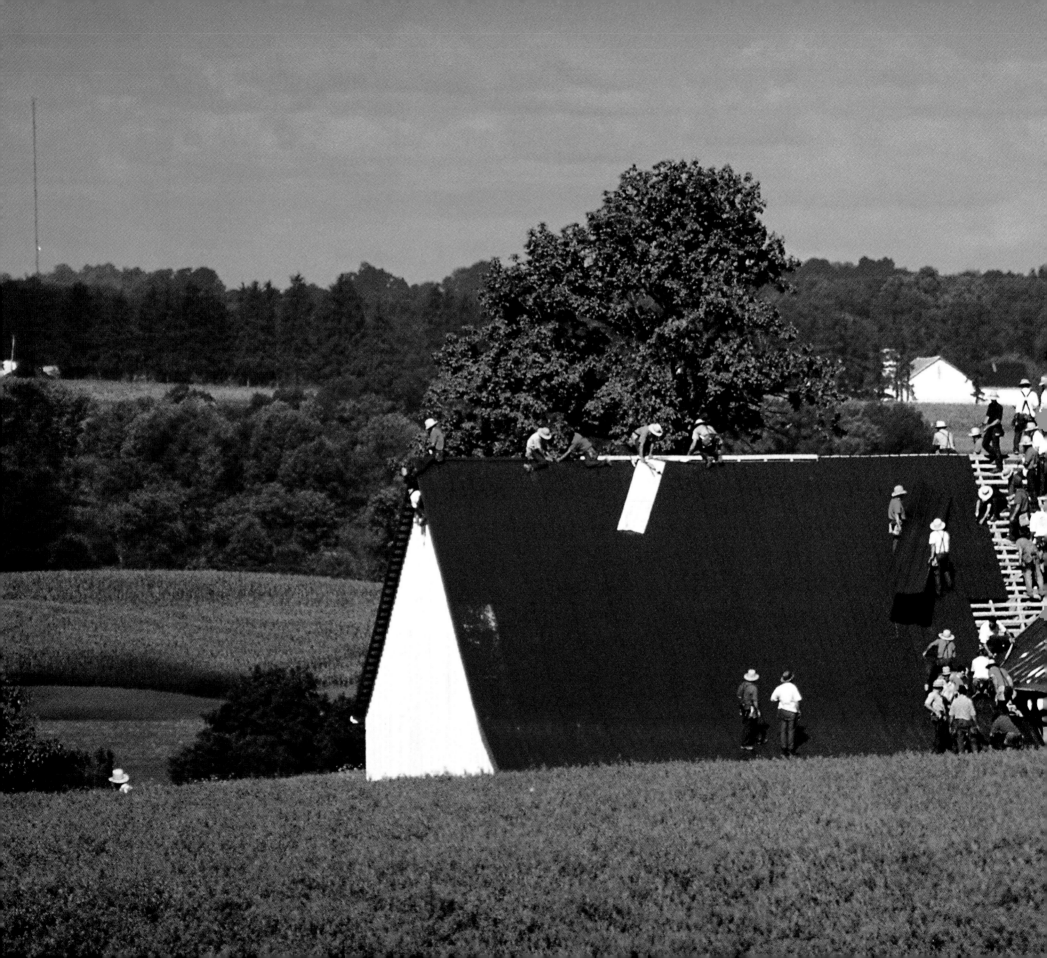

Opposite: "Sold, for $800! This quilt goes to number 236."

Previous Page: Many hands make light work.

Left: The tractor is already in its spot.

Below: This Amish family could have milked that evening if the equipment company had been available to install everything that day.

Benefit Auctions

This same effort to put the common good first is seen within the different churches. For example, the local Mennonite congregations host several charity auctions during the course of a year. One we attended was the Ohio Haiti Benefit Auction, which was a two-day event to raise money for Mennonite relief work in Haiti.

These benefit auctions are well-attended by Amish and Mennonites from Ohio and neighboring states, and are enormously successful. People bid generously on goods, knowing that their money will go to a worthwhile cause. Benefit auctions typically begin with a previewing of the goods to be sold, usually the night before the sale itself. These items include quilts, farm machinery, furniture, crafts,

and other collectable items. On the day of the auction, it is a packed, standing-room-only crowd under the enormous tent, bidding on goods.

Yet another feature of the weekend is the food tent, which features coffee, homemade pretzels and pastries in the morning, then a full chicken dinner, freshly baked pies, ice cream, and cider or lemonade for lunch.

Above: There is a variety of handmade quilts to choose from.

Left: An Amish family heads for the food tent.

Above: Ladies prepare a Mariner's Star quilt for the auction rack.

Left: Docks for unloading and picking up animals.

Below: On sale day a flea-market is held outside on the auction grounds.

Although a host of different events
are held at Mt. Hope Auction
throughout the year, its mainstay is
the weekly livestock auction every
Wednesday selling horses, cattle,
goats and sheep.

Left: A young Amish man demonstrates this horse's capabilities.

Elizabeth and Rosanna Miller

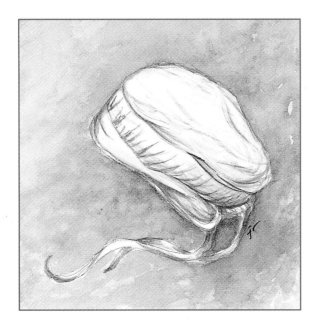

The Miller sisters are unconventional.

Rosie is Amish, and Betty is not. They love to travel, and together they have toured Europe, the United States, and Canada. They live together, and since Betty is not Amish, they are allowed electricity and a telephone. They both have jobs outside the home. While they have no children of their own (they are both unmarried), they do have twenty-three nieces and nephews.

Both Rosie and Betty have fond memories of their youth. There were eight children in their family, five girls and three boys. Rosie was fifth in line, Betty was the baby. Their family farmed and had fourteen or so cows that had to be milked by hand. While milking was a chore, the milking stable was also the best spot for gossiping. "If you wouldn't be out in the cow stable, you wouldn't find out the news," Rosie says.

Both women also remember the rigors of corn husking. Rosie enjoyed the husking as an activity and also loved the "good feeling" she got from finishing that task. Betty didn't enjoy the husking, but smiles at the memory of racing to find the Indian corn. "Our father would scatter the Indian corn amongst the field corn." Both also enjoyed the fact that during husking season, the kids would work hard, run in for lunch, and get to leave the kitchen without helping with the dishes.

They also recall the Snickers bars, the reward awaiting them for each row completed.

They attended a one-room schoolhouse until Rosie was in sixth grade, then they both went to a two-room schoolhouse, one room for lower grades, one room for upper grades. Their lower grade schoolteachers were Amish, and in the upper grades, they had a Mennonite teacher. They both remember admiring her outfits. "She had a new dress every day. She could go a whole week without having to wear the same dress twice." Looking back, they grimace when they think of how they wore the same dress several days in a row and drank out of a community water pail.

Food was basically homegrown. Instead of purchasing meat, or even taking their animals to be butchered, the Miller family slaughtered and prepared their own food-designated animals. They also did all of their own canning, baking, and berry picking. If there were any items they needed and couldn't provide for themselves, they shopped at The Country Mart in Mount Hope. A staple of their diet was soup. It was easy to prepare, inexpensive, and made a hearty, filling dinner.

Both Rosie and Betty are employed. Betty is a secretary at Troyer Gas, and for twelve years before that, she worked at Wayne Dalton, the garage door manufacturer in Mt. Hope. She loves the shorter hours and slower pace at Troyer Gas. In fact, after leaving Wayne Dalton, she kept mentioning to Rosie that the autumn leaves looked spectacular. She was so enthusiastic that Rosie finally figured out that Betty had not had a chance to see autumn leaves during the previous twelve years except on Sunday, due to the long hours she worked. Rosie works at the Killbuck Savings Bank. She has been there twenty years and her title is Assistant Vice President. She finds she loves the part of her job that involves working with people, but she does not enjoy the paperwork that goes along with it.

The sisters offer up valuable insights on common misconceptions about the Amish. "Sometimes people are surprised to find out we are just like they are," says Rosie. "Different beliefs make you who you are. People identify us by our clothes. It is not our clothes that make us who we are. What is in the heart is what matters!" Rosie continues. "You don't have to be Amish to be a Christian, nor are all Amish Christians. You can't have your clothes as a religion," she says.

Both enjoy the beauty and charm of the countryside. Winter is their favorite season; they love the slower pace and the view from their windows. They are also very connected to their family. After their father had a stroke in 1996, they would gather at the family farm on Sunday afternoons. Someone would always bring coffee and popcorn, and the

extended family would crowd into the small living room to share news about the events of the week. In the summer, the twenty-three nieces and nephews would play outside while the adults gathered. Rosie and Betty's father wouldn't say much, he'd just lean back in his rocker and listen, but all could tell he thoroughly enjoyed this family time.

Since their father's passing, they have continued this Sunday ritual for their mother. They also take turns cleaning their mother's house every Saturday. "We should probably clean on Mondays, after the mess we make on Sunday," joked Rosie, but their mother doesn't seem to mind.

Rosie and Betty Miller are proof that the role of women in Amish society is not, as many perceive, overly rigid. There is room for diversity. The sisters are spirited and honest, and in their way have gone outside tradition by not marrying and choosing to work. However, they are tied to Amish/Mennonite tradition by their love of family, commitment to a rigorous work ethic, and their adherence to faith.

Opposite: Amish children frolic and fish by a stream
on a warm summer day.

Right: Serenity

The Keims

Over lunch at a popular local eatery, Der Dutchman, we talked to business owner Bill Keim and his son Robbie. Both men are soft-spoken and unassuming, and the family resemblance is strong. They even share the same enormous grin and tendency to break into laughter.

Bill Keim was raised Amish, but he was never baptized into the Amish church. He attended public school until he was going into ninth grade, but only because there was no Amish school in the vicinity. When an Amish school was started in 1954, the year he was entering 9th grade, he switched over and attended that school for a year and a half. He left school at sixteen and started to work in the lumber yard his grandfather and great uncles had started in 1911. Even though he had entered the working world, Bill was still interested in getting his high school diploma, so he continued his schooling through the mail. However, the rigors of work made it impossible for him to complete his degree, and he found things like geometry difficult to learn. He reasoned that he didn't need geometry to price 2 x 4s, so he gave up his studies. It was also during this time that he left the Amish church altogether, becoming a member of the Mennonite church when he was twenty-one.

Bill enjoyed working at the family store. Originally, the store featured a planer and a feed grinder as well as selling hardware and

Left: Der Dutchman Restaurant.

ready-made doors. There was also lumber, though Bill points out that plywood didn't exist until the late 30s or early 40s. "I remember when plywood came out, and there was a place in Cleveland that stocked it. Once a week, my father would catch a ride with a guy who hauled livestock up to Cleveland. After they delivered the livestock, they had to clean out the truck before they could load it up with plywood."

During the time he worked at his family store, Bill lived at home. In fact, he lived at home for many years, and everyone had him pegged as a confirmed bachelor. He surprised them all by marrying Carolyn when he was twenty-nine. The couple waited six years to have children. Then, they had four - Robbie, Maria, Heather, and Bethany. When Carolyn was forty-four (Robbie was twelve at the time) she

passed away after a struggle with cancer. Bill eventually met and married Eva, who had two children, Eric and Kim, from a previous marriage.

The small family business became what is today Keim Lumber, a thriving lumberyard, mill, and building supplier. Keim Lumber has grown from a small operation with a couple of buildings, limited products, and two employees to a huge business with many acres of warehouses and facilities and over two hundred employees. Even with economic slow-downs, the lumberyard has continued to prosper. Keim Lumber does not manufacture products for tourists per se, though they do create hard wood moldings and other supplies for tourist-oriented shops, so the fact that tourism is the fastest growing business in Holmes County only affects Keim's business indirectly.

Both Bill and Robbie see the pros and cons of the growing tourist trade. From an economic viewpoint, "Tourists are good, but sometimes you have people you wouldn't want" coming into the community, Robbie says.

They both recall a time when bed and breakfast inns were a rarity. Bill recalls a friend who rented out her spare bedroom as "a way to make a bit of extra cash." Now, "there are so many bed and breakfasts that they are almost falling over each other."

Both men laugh at some of the misconceptions about the Amish. "Tourists expect to see hex signs, but they exist only in Pennsylvania," laughed Robbie. "Also, many tourists regard the Amish as only objects to take pictures of, but they are really just

like anybody else. In fact, they are quite gifted craftsmen and talented in many other areas." Both men have many friends among the Amish.

Bill relayed a story about a group of tourists who came in and showed no respect at all for the Amish prohibition against taking photographs. "They acted as if they were at a zoo, snapping shots of whatever was in the next cage." For the most part, though, both see the benefits of tourism, and say tourists are by and large respectful and interested in the Amish community.

Bill enjoys the change of seasons. From a work standpoint, summer is his favorite season, because they are the busiest. He used to worry that in the winter, they wouldn't have enough work for all the men, and he would find himself wishing that they would all just stay home until spring. The work has picked up to such an extent that he no longer worries about that. Robbie is partial to fall. He likes both the slowing pace of work and the dramatic colors of the foliage. Both Bill and Robbie are tied to their work and their community. They both recall Bill's dad's motto, "buy low, sell high." Even though this is the most basic economic rule of thumb, they also acknowledge that their success goes much deeper than financial logic. Bill credits "tithing and supporting missions." He feels that this is important, "especially during the tough times." He feels that God honors this. "The money is not ours. We are only the stewards of it. You can do good or bad things with the money. If you do good things with it, God gives you opportunities to do more good things."

Robbie is quick to add a lesson he learned from his dad. "Dad taught me to be truthful. If you order something and you are under or overcharged, it's up to you to tell them. Then, you don't have to worry about it, because you did the right thing."

The credo at Keim Lumber is "high quality and service." Bill and Robbie Keim exemplify this high quality and attention to the service of God and others not only in business but also in their everyday life.

Eli and Lydia Ann Bowman

Eli Bowman and his wife, Lydia Ann, live on a small farm outside the town of Mount Hope. They are in their sixties, physically very different from each other, but are somehow utterly complimentary in their differences. Lydia Ann has a kind face and silver hair, and seems full of down-to-earth dignity. She dresses in typical Amish fashion, with a dark, solid fabric dress and a head covering. Eli wears suspenders, a button-down collared shirt, and the beard one might expect of an Amish man, but there is something disarmingly elfin about him. He has a permanent glint in his eye, and he doesn't ever sit still for long.

Their home is plain in certain respects, but Eli is a collector so there weren't the pristine cleared surfaces that I had seen in other Amish homes. There were books and souvenirs about, and many of the pieces of furniture were heirlooms, complete with stories about when they were made and by whom. Eli and Lydia Ann have four grown children, Dan, Paul, Ervin, and Barbara, and six grandchildren, two of whom were being cared for by Lydia Ann the day we came to visit.

Eli and Lydia Ann met when Eli was eighteen and Lydia Ann was twenty. They dated for three years before getting married. Eli came from a family of ten children, five boys and five girls.

Lydia Ann grew up with seven brothers and four sisters. Lydia Ann recalls her childhood responsibility of carrying the water buckets from the well to the house, no matter what the weather. Eli helped with many of the chores around his family farm. One of his earliest memories is that of the weekly bath ritual. He would share the same wooden tub with his brother, bathing in a mixture of cold water direct from the well and hot water, which had been boiled over the fire. "I always fought to use the tub first," Eli says with a laugh. "After a week of running around outdoors on the farm, we were both pretty dirty, and I wanted to get into that water while it was still somewhat warm and clean."

The house they live in now is comparatively new. They built it in 1961, but it was actually nothing more than a covered basement for the first eight years. They lived in four small underground rooms during that period, and both remember the flood of 1969. One morning, after a night of torrential rain, Eli recalls climbing out of bed. "I put my feet down only to find that I was sloshing through several inches of water." Shortly after that, they began construction of their home above ground.

Right now, Eli works at Wayne Dalton, garage door manufacturer and the largest employer in the area. In term of years, he said he has "given half his life" (over thirty-five years) to Wayne Dalton.

Before working there, he worked a number of jobs, all for the pay rate of approximately one dollar per hour. He has chipped ice, farmed, and even went about getting odd jobs during a spell when he was out of steady employment. His job at Wayne Dalton these days consists of painting wooden garage doors that are shipped world wide. At this point, he claims to know the workings of the factory so well, he can tell the minute a pump breaks or when the paint guns aren't working properly. They have three sons, Dan, Ervin and Paul, and one daughter, Barbara. Dan has a shop across the street from Eli and Lydia Ann's house. He sells and repairs tractors and lawn mowers. Ervin is employed by Wayne Dalton and lives close by with his wife Mable and their two children. Paul is also employed by Wayne Dalton and currently lives at home. Their daughter Barbara lives very close by as well, and her husband David is a carpenter.

Eli and Lydia Ann seem quite happy and comfortable together. Lydia Ann teased Eli very gently about his propensity to talk at length, and laughed every time he bounded up from his chair to show us some gadget or novelty item he created and tried to market. There was his hairbrush for bald men (just a handle, no bristles), a wooden oven pan puller, and Amish coloring books. He has also compiled, written, edited and produced *Mount Hope: A Pictorial History*, which is, as the title suggests, an extensive study of Mount Hope.

He was able to pour his love of history and genealogy into this project. He gave us a copy of this impressive volume, which was beautifully bound and quite comprehensive.

Where did he get the time to work on it? At night, Lydia Ann told us, is when Eli loves to "do his writing, his research, and his work with wood, not to mention his fascination with his model trains." What does Lydia Ann do? "Well," she said. "I like to play a game once in a while. Cards or things of that nature. But usually Eli is too intent on a project to play. Lots of times I quilt." In fact, that night an enormous and beautiful quilt in progress was in a frame in the living room, and Lydia Ann was expecting Dan's wife Anna over to work on it that evening. They would work by the bright light of one large gas lamp.

It was fascinating to see the way Eli and Lydia Ann balanced as a couple. Together, they complete the equation that I see as successful for the Amish way of life. Eli has the boundless energy and dogged work ethic, and the resourceful way of looking at the world with ingeniousness and industriousness. He is always trying to find ways to do things better within the teachings and customs of Amish society. "If he weren't Amish, he would be the CEO of a global corporation," was my observation. Lydia Ann, on the other hand, represents the slower pace, the ability to delight in the rhythms of the natural world around her, and the values of home, in a classic sense. Together, they achieve an ideal harmony.

Above: This coat is for the cool morning ride.

Above: Smoke curls from the chimney of this typical Amish home.

Pennsylvania Dutch

Originally, the Amish people came from Switzerland, France, and Germany, so one might reasonably expect that the Amish might speak several different languages. However, despite the fact that the Amish came from three countries, their points of origin all fall within the same Alemannic dialect range. In the United States, this dialect is commonly referred to as Pennsylvania Dutch. This is not to identify the dialect in any way as coming from the Netherlands, but rather, "Dutch" is a folk rendering of the term "Deitsch," or German.

Basically, the Amish speak three distinct languages. First, they can read, write and speak English, which they do at school or when they are out in the world. Then, they speak Pennsylvania Dutch (which is primarily an oral language and the one with which they are most comfortable) at home and in social settings with other Amish. They also have a knowledge of High German, since that is the language used in their Bible, sermons, and all ceremonial occasions. When mingling with the "English," which is what they call any person from outside the community, they will speak English, often without an accent. However, this is not to say that English is their primary language. In fact, many Amish children speak only Pennsylvania Dutch until they enter school.

The Pennsylvania Dutch dialect is a very important part of Amish community gatherings. Most of the Amish social life, the visits, singings, sales, barn-raisings, and frolics, involve much conversation, and the primary language that the Amish converse in is Pennsylvania Dutch. Their language reinforces the bonds of community and identity they share.

Right: Home is where the heart is…no matter what language you speak.

Above: Throughout the year, Amish and Mennonites alike gather together for fellowship and fun.
Above Right: Two young Mennonite boys.
Right: Hold that egg steady!

Phraseology

One bit of phraseology that I heard in Holmes County was the way in which families are designated. In most places, there are so many different surnames that families can be identified merely by a last name. However, in Holmes County, with such large families and so few last names (for example, 27% of the Old Order Amish families in Ohio have Miller as a last name, and 17% are Yoders), one could not say, "The Millers are coming for dinner"- that could mean any one of over 500 families.

Families are designated by first names within a family unit, and first name and last name outside the family. So, if brother Eli and his family are coming for Sunday dinner, a family member would say, "Elis are coming at noon." If speaking of someone outside the immediate family, one would say, "Eli Millers are coming at noon." Of course, there are probably many Eli Millers in Holmes County, so the designation narrows by adding the appropriate middle initial, as in "Eli J. Millers are coming for dinner."

In and around town...

Below: In the heart of Berlin.

Above and Right: Popular tourist spots to shop.

The Budget

The Budget is a weekly newspaper, published in the town of Sugarcreek. While it contains all the local news, it also, as it proclaims on its masthead, "serves the Amish Mennonite Communities throughout the Americas." While it is interesting and informative to read the local news, with its fairly standard articles about new computers, high school sports teams, and even national economic trends and how they are affecting the local economy, the most enjoyable reading comes from scribes located in Amish and Mennonite communities in the United States and abroad.

For example, here is an excerpt from a letter written by Edward and Rachel Martin, of Alta Vista, Iowa: "On Wed. we three sisters-in-law got together to make noodles and soap while the dairy men went to a meeting in Elma. Since I didn't need noodles and had all the ingredients for laundry soap, I made soap in Marlene's furnace kettle. She kindly cut it out for me, now I should go fetch it to get it out of her way." Or, this bit from a Mennonite community in Brooten, Minnesota, courtesy of Mrs. Carleton Zimmerman: "There was a stir in the neighborhood the other week. While a neighbor

was shelling corn, a little over a mile to the west of us, a bear ran out of the field and climbed a tree. This is not bear country. They are pretty thick further north."

Also in *The Budget* you'll find detailed obituaries, and numerous advertisements for things such as wood burning stoves, gas lamps, livestock, and quilts. News of impending weddings, baby's births, and illnesses are also included. A look at *The Budget* offers a fascinating glimpse into the hard-working daily lives of the Amish and Mennonites. It's an old-fashioned, simpler way of life, both innocent and charming. *The Budget*, with its features, stories, and scribes' letters, provides a window into what makes the Amish and Mennonite people tick. What stands out repeatedly is a commitment to God, family, and fellowship.

Above: The Amish Door Inn
Left: Carlisle Village Inn

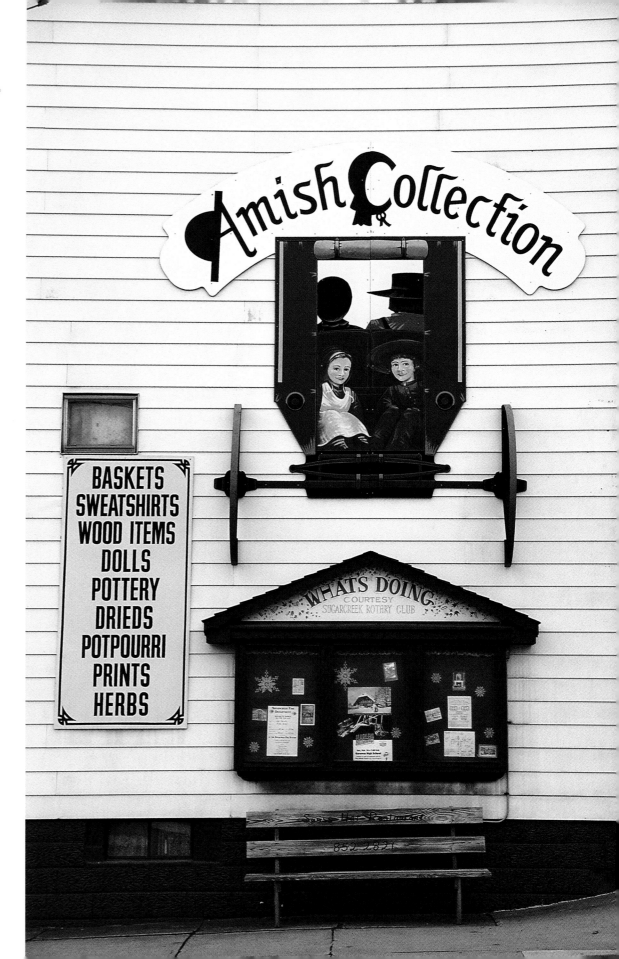

Right: What's 'Doing' in Sugarcreek?

Above: Coblentz Chocolates

Above: Winter sunset.

Left: Shopping for produce.

Right: Der Bake Oven in Berlin.

By Hand

BY HAND

In the modern world, most of the labor we do is with the help of technology. While sophisticated machinery makes the work much swifter and more efficient, some of the joy of creation is lost when you shorten the amount of time spent in making an object or performing a task, and one also misses the direct involvement that is part of working with one's hands.

In Holmes County, the love of creating work by hand- and the ability to do that work- has not been lost. Whether in farming, carpentry or crafts, individuals put their unique mark on what they do, largely because they have done the work on their own. Hand plows, hand saws, needles for sewing, everything is accomplished in real time through personal effort, without the distance created by machines.

"...Self-sufficiency, fellowship and tradition."

Farming, when done by hand, puts the farmer directly in touch with the soil. Whether walking behind a hand-held plow or guiding a team of horses behind a hay baler, one gets a true feel for the earth and the way things grow. Similarly, when working with wood when one cuts and carves a piece of wood by hand, rather than taking pre-cut wood and placing it on a machine for further refinement, it is possible to experience the visceral feeling of working with an element and seeing and feeling it take shape.

Below: Field corn for the animals.

"The Lord your God has blessed you in all the work of your hands."

- Deut. 2:7

When work is done by hand, there is a reality and concreteness to the finished product, the pace of life slows down. Humans can only work so fast. There is less uniformity but more care and beauty in each unique piece. The Amish and Mennonite communities put their mark on the items they produce, be it cheese or corn or furniture.

There is an awareness that a natural substance was transformed or nurtured by the efforts of an individual possessing a particular skill or training. The handiwork that results from this bonds them to their philosophy of self-sufficiency, fellowship, and tradition.

Left: Comradery

"Lazy hands make a man poor, but diligent hands bring wealth."

- Proverbs 10:4

J.R. Schrock

Mid-winter, early morning in Holmes County. The sunrise glints off the magical silver ice crystal webs covering the treetops. We drive over snow-covered roads to The Wooden Toy Shop, the thriving business owned by Alvin Schrock, Jr., commonly called J.R.

J.R. is a soft-spoken man. In his face are both industriousness and a calm intelligence. He is quick to smile and laugh, and despite the bustle of activity in his shop, there is nothing frantic or pressured about the atmosphere there. Shelves running the length, depth, and virtually the height of the building are stocked with an astounding variety of wooden toys and decorative pieces. Most of these items were carefully sanded, stained, and varnished. We saw magazine holders, stick horses, wooden puzzles, bookcases, dolls and doll furniture, baskets, picture frames...the list goes on and on. His most popular item? We tried to guess, but finally he had to tell us: a roll-top breadbasket.

We had just seen J.R. in church the previous day, and we asked about his family. His eyes light up when he talks about them. J.R. and his wife Rhoda have four children, Austin, Rachelle, Erik, and Trevor. Clearly enthusiastic about our visit, he asked us if we'd like to see his workshop. We followed him out across the driveway to an adjacent building. Stepping inside, we found

Above: Left to Right Austin, Rachelle, Erik and Trevor.

ourselves in a tidy woodworking shop, equipped with a variety of electric power saws and drills. The floor was swept clean of dust and scraps, and we watched as an older Amish man sitting at a band saw worked steadily and carefully. Nearby, an Amish teenager was working at a small drill.

"I bought this shop from Al, an Amish fellow," J.R. told us. "Without using electricity, he found he couldn't grow the business, so he thought about it and decided it made more sense to sell it to me. Just think, it took him twenty minutes to half and hour to light the fifteen gas lamps that used to be the only source of light the shop had. Now, we have thirty florescent lights illuminating the same space. Also, the previous owner ran a line shaft under the boards of

Left: Practiced hands.

the floor, which was attached outside to a diesel engine, then connected by pulleys to each machine. Well, I knew that system could be improved upon, so within six months after I bought the shop, I re-wired and rearranged everything for maximum efficiency." It was clear to us, as we walked around the shop, that J.R. had optimally used every bit of space and light to the workers' advantage.

"Some things haven't changed from the old days," he told us. "The common thread would be attention to fine craftsmanship and detail."

What inspired him to take on this company, we ask? "I love wood and always have," he tells us. "I grew up working with wood." We watch as he points to the types of wood in the shop and names

them all- oak, walnut, cherry, maple. "Here in the shop, we mainly use oak. It's a hard, sturdy wood, and the largest market we have is for things made of oak."

We enter a side room of the workshop, and see several Amish girls and one Amish boy busily sanding doll-size high chairs. As they worked, they laughed and spoke to each other in Pennsylvania Dutch, not even pausing in their work as we came in. J.R. looked over their finished pieces and smiled his approval. As we left, he turned to us and said quietly, "With the finishing, I don't know what it is, but the girls just seem to do better than the guys. More attention to detail, maybe, they are used to cleaning things up at home and making things shiny." J.R. told us he hires the girls at age fourteen or

fifteen, when they leave school, and they generally work there until they get married.

J.R. also hires the handicapped from a neighboring special-needs school. These mentally and physically challenged workers, all Amish, assemble many of the wooden items. This speaks volumes about J.R.'s compassion and very real commitment to the Amish community. The relationship he has with his workers is one of mutual respect, and the relationship he has with the Amish community at large is based on wanting his neighbors and employees to share in his good fortune. He does not merely run a successful business for his own personal gain. Of the eighteen workers he employs, only two are not Amish. He praises their work ethic and efficiency.

When we leave The Wooden Toy Shop, it all seems pretty clear. This is the way a small business should be run. Organized, productive, hiring people to capitalize on their different skills but all from within the community. J.R. runs The Wooden Toy Shop with his head and his heart. I would say his most important thing emerging from his shop is not a roll-top breadbasket, but the respect and very real sense of community he fosters.

Above: Amish dolls – notice they do not have faces.

Monroe and Ida Mast

Right next door to J.R. Schrock's Wooden Toy Shop is the home of the shop foreman, Monroe. It's a traditional Amish home or, in other words, a very simple two-story dwelling, painted white and without shutters or any other type of adornment. Right next to Monroe's house is the home of his brother, Merle, who also works at the Toy Shop. Their father, Al, was the original owner of the shop.

Monroe has been married to his wife Ida for seven years. They have four children: Maynard, Marcus, Mary Beth, and a baby, Julia. Maynard is six years old and the only one of the children in school. Part of his walking route to school is along a busy road, but Maynard, often accompanied by a neighbor's older child, has been walking or riding his bike along that route (school is a mile away) and Ida doesn't worry at all.

We walked in and saw the two middle children, five-year-old Marcus and three year-old Mary Beth, sitting on the sofa and playing quietly. Baby Julia was sleeping in her crib in an adjoining bedroom. The children are beautiful, both neatly dressed in traditional Amish clothing, though Mary Beth rebelled a bit about wearing her head-covering (ultimately, her mother prevailed and she put it on).

At home, they speak Pennsylvania Dutch, though they speak English at school. In fact, one of the games the children play at home is school, and teaching English reading words is part of the game.

Monroe and Ida's home is slightly different from a typical Amish home. They have limited electricity. The reason they are allowed electricity is that Mary Beth was diagnosed with cystic fibrosis. Monroe and Ida appealed to the leaders of their church, requesting that they have the electricity run in so they could have air conditioning in the summer (Mary Beth found it almost impossible to breathe in the heat and humidity) and also so they could hook in the machine Mary Beth must use to break up the build-up in her lungs twice a day. They do not seem at all devastated by Mary Beth's illness or prognosis. Instead, they are cheerfully determined to work together to keep her comfortable and as healthy as possible.

Monroe and Ida first met at a church youth group hymn singing. Ida comes from a family of eleven children. She is the middle child. Her family lives only eleven miles away, yet she rarely gets a chance to see them. A trip of this length by horse and buggy is very significant; there is no hopping into a car. They grow their own tomatoes, potatoes, cabbage, corn, and lettuce. Their crop is sufficient for their family, with enough left over to sell to a local farm market.

Left: Marcus and Mary Beth.

Ida shops very carefully once a month or so, going by van with other Amish wives to local stores. If there is an emergency item she runs out of mid-month, J.R. will often get things for her.

What is an average evening like for the Mast family? Usually, Ida helps Maynard with his schoolwork, and then they have a simple supper (the example Ida gave me was hamburger, mashed potatoes, and whatever vegetable was in season) after which she cleans up. As a family, they often read Bible stories and sing. The children go to bed quite early, and more often than not, Ida and Monroe are in bed by nine.

With shy graciousness, Ida asked if I'd like to see the bedrooms upstairs. We went first to her room, and she showed us the beautiful quilt her mother had made for her as a wedding gift. The adjoining room was Maynard's and Marcus's room, and I was struck by the total lack of clutter. There were no posters or stacks of baseball cards or mountains of plastic toys. Instead, there was the bed and a dresser. "The kids have only what they need," she told me. "Nothing more." I was struck by the fact that I was walking through a house with three children under the age of five. No fighting, no yelling, no din from a television set.

Just as we were leaving, Monroe came to check in on his family and to see about lunch. Even though they weren't physically demonstrative, there was a strong tacit bond between husband and wife. Amazing to think, here was a young family, with a serious illness omnipresent, but you would never know it. All you feel at work in that quiet, uncluttered home is love and faith and hope. Monroe kisses Mary Beth's head and she beams.

Noah and Mary Troyer

Noah and Mary Troyer live on a farm east of Berlin, Ohio. Mary grew up on this particular farm. In fact, her grandparents moved there in 1912, when Mary's father was six. Mary runs the house and cared for their six children, four boys and two girls, all of whom are now grown. Noah has two vocations: he farms (his crops are corn and hay, and he also had milking cows for twenty-eight years) and he raises exotic animals. He has a large variety of unusual animals, including peacocks, emus, llamas, miniature horses, and Watusi cattle. This does not sound like your typical Amish home!

Mary was one of the six girls in her family. All of the girls helped with the work around her parents' farm, since there were no boys. She attended a nearby one-room schoolhouse, and even went so far as to take extra schooling past eighth grade, all the way through tenth grade. For her last two years, though, she only went to school on Saturdays since the public school used the school building during the week.

Noah grew up near the town of Sugarcreek. He was one of fourteen children. His mother died at the age of forty-nine when his youngest sibling was only three-years old. Like Mary, he too completed tenth grade, but he went to a public school since there was no Amish school in the vicinity. Noah attended school just after World War II, and he was teased a great deal, largely because of the Conscientious Objector status that the Amish have. He recalls that when they played basketball at school, no one would pass to the Amish if they could help it. "I was afraid to go to school at one point, because a neighborhood boy whose house I had to pass by threatened me one day with a butcher knife. His family had three boys in the service and they didn't like Amish." Looking back on this, he says he realizes that the taunting and threats he heard from some children was simply them repeating what they heard at home.

Mary and Noah are happy with their lives. When asked if she would like a new house, Mary shakes her head. "I like my home. I wouldn't trade it. All my memories are here." She doesn't even mind the round of chores she does, from Monday's laundry to Saturday's cooking. "I don't mind any of the days. When you have health, it is no problem. Health is a good gift." She says this last sentence rather wistfully, as she has been ill of late. Noah, too, enjoys his home and his work,

especially his exotic animal business. He does, however, notice some changes in the Amish community. "In the last ten years, there has been a great change. There is not enough land for everyone to farm, so some Amish have taken seven to three thirty jobs (we'd call them nine to five jobs!). These people have smaller properties which take less time to keep up, so they have more leisure time." As a result of this, he sees a change in the work ethic of Amish youth. "Children who grow up in these homes don't have the same chores as children who live on farms. Also, shopping has increased, because these families don't have the land or the time to grow their own food."

Mary and Noah still feel the ties they have to the land and the seasons. Mary loves the spring "when everything is sprouting out." Noah agrees. "It is a time of new life. Uplifting is a word that comes to mind." They both love the autumn, too. Mary loves to go out in the fall to see all of the fall colors, and Noah says, "As a farmer, your crops are in and you know you have adequate provisions for winter. There's nothing like a full barn!"

The values Noah and Mary have strived to pass down to their children come from the Bible. First, "Love the Lord your God with all your heart and all your soul and all your mind." Then, secondly, "Love your neighbor as yourself." Content and at peace, Mary and Noah, in their simple farmhouse, live these principles every day.

Inset: Emu

On the farm...

Above: Protector

Left: Stability through the good
and bad times.

Right: Grooming

Left: Four-legged lawn mower.

Right: "Come and git it!"

This farmer stacks his hay (on left, used to feed animals) and straw (on right, the animals bedding) loosely, by using a system of steel hooks and pulleys (pictured left) to raise large quantities at a time into position.

Left: Windmills are still used today to draw water from wells.

Seasons

The cycle of the seasons defines Holmes County. Since it is rural and largely agricultural, much of what goes on there is a direct result of the elements. When we talked to Holmes County residents about their favorite season, we were interested to discover that many liked several different times of the year equally. Try as they might, they could not limit themselves to one favorite season.

What many people expressed was their love of the cycle of changing seasons within the year, appreciating fully not only specific seasonal attributes but the gentle shifts as each passing season buds, blossoms, and fades. This interest in and love of natural seasonal cycles is, I think, rather like embracing the journey as well as the destination.

Previous Page: Fall colors blanket the rolling hills.
Opposite: A young Amish man leans back on the reins of his spirited work horses.

"...embracing the journey as well as the destination."

Spring in Holmes County changes from the pale green and muted earth tones to full-out emerald hills and rich, newly plowed fertile brown soil as it progresses from late March to May. In the spring, the fields are filled with farmers planting their crops. The winding roads are lined with daffodils and blossoming trees, and the grass turns from sparse and drab to lush as soon as the weather warms. It is a busy time of the year for farmers, but all seem to enjoy being out in the fresh air with a warming sun beating down, or in the damp misty gray of a cloudy day where you can almost feel the crops grow.

Even those Amish and Mennonites who do not make their living by farming almost without exception enjoy planting small gardens of flowers and vegetables.

Above: Relaxation

Above: Narrow roads create unusual sights as old and new worlds intersect

Opposite: Early morning tranquility.

Right: It's the simple things.

Summer is hot, but not unbearably so. The pace of life slows down a bit, and while crops are tended to, with school and planting not in the picture, there is time to enjoy a swim in the swimming hole, eat an ice cream cone, or just find a cool spot under the welcome shade of a tree. The days are long, and the vivid sunsets over the ripening fields are nothing short of spectacular. There are more tourists around in the summer, creating more traffic and more noise but boosting the local economy.

"There is a time for everything,
and a season for every activity under heaven."
- **Ecclesiastes 3:1**

Above: Horsing around at the feed wagon.

Opposite: Field of dreams.

Fall's colors are dramatic. Early on, the fields hold onto their green while the adjacent trees are ablaze with color. Again, there is a frenzy of activity for the farmers. This time, it is harvesting, rather than planting, which takes up their time.

Older children are called upon to help in the fields before or after school. Everyone we spoke to seems to love the fall vistas and drives by car or buggy through the countryside to see the fall colors.

Right: "Ich bedank mich Gott fa da goot eahnd."

Left: Field corn for the cattle.

Above: The days are getting shorter as winter approaches.

Winter is a quiet season. Thoughts and activities turn inward. From the warmth of their toasty kitchens and comfortable living rooms, the residents of Holmes County look out at the stark white, frozen terrain. With their pantries full, they seem to enjoy this dormant season, a period of rest. The countryside looks magical with a coating of white, which causes the dark buggies and red barns to stand out in contrast. Smoke curls from chimneys and frost adorns trees.

Left: These corn shocks shocked by hand hearken back to a pre-industrial age.

"He leads me beside quiet waters. He restores my soul."
- Psalms 23:2-3

The seasons in Holmes County are cherished and appreciated as being part of a larger cycle of growth, ripeness, death, and rebirth.

Right: A New Idea manure spreader sits protected underneath the barn.

Pranks

As in other communities, the month of October gives rise to pranks. Some are fairly standard - for example, toilet papering trees - but one prank in particular stands out as nothing short of amazing.

One October morning, in Mount Hope, residents woke to find eight buggies on the top of the roof of the grocery store. No one could fathom how the buggies got there, until it was time to figure out how to get them down. At that point, one young boy suggested using two enormous garage door panels that were leaning against the building as a ramp up to the roof and rolling the perched buggies down. It was at that point that it was noticed that the garage doors already had wheel tracks on them! What went up, then came down, using the same method, and the mystery, though no one ever admitted to the prank, was solved.

Left: An honor system vegetable and fruit stand.

Above: Pumpkins and Gourds for sale.

Funerals

Within the Amish and Mennonite communities, death is treated with great reverence. While it is a time for reflection and sorrow, it is seen as a natural part of the cycle of life. They are not losing their family members forever, but will simply need to wait for their reunion in Heaven. For both groups, funerals are not elaborate affairs.

For the Mennonites, a funeral service is conducted in a church, with a funeral procession driving to the cemetery, similar to a funeral in many Christian communities. The gravesite is designated by a simple marker.

For the Amish, however, a local funeral parlor might be involved with the embalming, and the deceased person would be viewed at their home. After three days, the body is placed in a plain wooden coffin, which is then put on the back of an open wagon and a funeral procession of buggies files out to the cemetery. There is a very brief service at the gravesite (which is dug by family members and members of the congregation), after which the coffin is lowered. The gravesite is marked with a simple piece of sandstone which is made and engraved by one of their own. Many of the cemeteries are bordered by a small fence.

Above: A new Amish gravesite.

Ron and Sheri Miller

Ron and Sheri Miller live on a beautiful piece of wooded property with a view of farmland pastures and rolling hills. Their home is new and compact. They welcomed us into their cozy living room.

Ron and Sheri are Mennonites, so they have electricity and all the modern conveniences in their home. In the living room, the bookshelves are full of books and an assortment of videos. On the wall hangs a gallery of family portraits. There are also many toys and blankets in evidence, which belong to their young son, Magnus. Magnus is a fair-skinned, blue-eyed tot with an easygoing personality and expansive smile.

Ron is a master carpenter, and when Sheri took us on a tour of their home, she showed us the bedroom set Ron made. He fashioned the set while a student in high school. The bed and dressers are solid oak, highly polished, intricate in detail while at the same time very solid in construction. Ron actually went to a state competition with one of the pieces when he was in high school. His shop class and teacher were the defining elements of his high school education.

Above: Recess at an Amish school.

Ron was raised Amish until he entered grade school. At that time, his family became Mennonites. While his parents now are not conservative Mennonites, Ron is. Ron grew up in the town of Sugarcreek. He doesn't remember too much of his young life before leaving the Amish church, but he does recall that the Amish kids were sometimes poked fun of at school, and remembers how happy he was to change his style of dress and use electricity. The home Ron and Sheri live in now is directly across the street from Ron's grandmother's farm, which is a typical Amish farmhouse with a main home and "dauti haus," or grandparent's house next door, where the older generation moves when the next generation takes over the farm. The land Ron and Sheri's home sits on was purchased from Ron's parents.

Sheri is the youngest of Eli and Marcella Wengerd's six children, and the only girl. She has a straight-forward, relaxed approach to life, perhaps because she grew up as the only girl in a house full of boys. She is a bit more direct and assertive than several of the other Mennonite women we met, and she has many tales to tell about being teased mercilessly by the three brothers closest to her in age, and how her eldest brothers always defended her. She is still "very close, despite the teasing" to her brothers, and sees her parents frequently. Sheri works at home, sewing Amish coats for her parent's shop, in addition to caring for Magnus and doing all the cooking, laundry, and cleaning involved in running a house. According to everyone asked, Sheri makes "the world's best cheesecake." Sheri, Ron, and Magnus eat together every night. Sheri prepares simple, hearty food (one dish she mentioned as being a family favorite is "Tatertot Casserole"). Sheri and Ron don't watch television, though Sheri will occasionally watch an exercise video. "T.V. was never a part of my life, so it doesn't occur to me to think of it, much less miss it," she says.

Ron and Sheri have known each other virtually their entire lives. As teenagers, they would go out with the same group of four close friends from their church, and Ron was a good friend of Sheri's older brother Myron. "I liked Sheri from the first time we met," Ron says, with a smile on his face. In fact, Ron approached Sheri's father and asked if it would be all right if he started dating Sheri. Eli's response was that it was fine with him, but he felt Ron's biggest challenge would be getting Sheri to agree. Sheri loved Ron's friendship but didn't want to extend their relationship beyond that. After a while, with the help of Ron and Myron's subtle encouragement, Sheri began to go out with Ron, and they dated for a year before becoming married.

Both Sheri and Ron are very active in the church. Ron has an excellent voice and sings in the same Men's Chorus as Sheri's father and brothers. Sheri attends Bible study and quilting circles, and the family is in attendance for every Sunday sermon without fail. "I can't see us living a city life," Sheri says. "I'm very happy with the community here." Before becoming a mother, Sheri was a monitor at a private Christian school, and when she thinks about educating Magnus, she thinks they will either home school him or send him to a Christian school. Ron, Sheri and Magnus lead a simple life. When in their presence, a strong sense of love and contentment is pervasive. Ron and Sheri are good friends. Ron does not have to be reminded to attend to his son, or to help Sheri around the house; he naturally wants to do those things. Both seem happiest when playing with Magnus, who is clearly the light of their lives.

Right: Golden maple.

Jemima Wengerd

Jemima Wengerd was born in 1919 in Wayne County. There were eight children in her family. One baby was stillborn, and she had two brothers and four sisters. When Jemima was eight, her nine-year-old sister died. Then, only one year later when Jemima was nine, her mother, Katie Ann, died at the age of thirty-eight. At the time, Jemima's oldest sibling was sixteen. The family struggled along until three years later, when Jemima's father married Katie Ann's sister.

Jemima, as was the custom for all Amish teens, was involved in an Amish youth fellowship. The young people of the church would typically gather on Sunday evenings. One Sunday night, they happened to be at the home of a young man named Jacob Wengerd. A group of Amish girls were descending the stairs when Jake looked up. One girl captured his attention, and Jake claims he knew then and there that Jemima was the girl he was going to marry. And so it was. Jemima married Jacob J. Wengerd on December 8, 1938. Interestingly, Jemima's maiden name was also Wengerd, though they were not related. Her husband worked as a farmer and at various times as a mechanic. Shortly after the wedding, Jake hired himself out to work on a farm. They owned one cow and Jemima brought twelve chickens from home. The cow provided enough milk so that Jemima was able to churn it into butter to sell.

The couple had four daughters, Katie Ann, Ada, Emma, and Edna, and one son, Eli. Up until 1947, they raised their children Amish, but at that point, began to attend a Beachy Amish church, and they bought a car. Amish preachers came into their home and asked the Wengerd's why they were going to the Beachy church and why they had an automobile. Jake told them, "A car is like any other piece of machinery. It is not the car that is the problem, but what you do with it. You can do wrong with a horse and buggy." Shortly after this, the family moved and Jemima decided it was time to learn how to drive. She recalls a time Jake asked her to drive to Millersburg on an errand. She was in the car with a friend, who had just learned how to drive also and had taken the wheel. As they were driving along a one-way street, the gas pedal fell off. Thankfully, some nice men at a gas station came to their rescue and re-attached the pedal so they could get home.

On the day we visited her in the homey, two-bedroom basement apartment she occupies in her daughter Katie Ann's home, Jemima was quilting. The comforter which had been pieced earlier was set up in a frame. We watched as she attached the batting and backing to the top, deftly using an x-stitch pattern with such skill and ease that it seemed as if she could do it in her sleep. Most comforters are done with a knot in the center or corner of each block, but on this particular one it was decided to complete it with a set of diagonal cross-stitches. Quilting is one of her favorite activities. When she finishes a quilt, she brings it to the local quilt store for them to sell. The quilt on her own bed is a gift from her dear friends. She and Jake had been helping out a family with several daughters. One day, she happened to be at the family's house, and she lent a hand with their quilting. While they sewed, she told the girls that she would like a quilt just like the one they were making. Jake overheard her and went back to order one for her. She loved it, but didn't want to use it until her daughters encouraged her to put it on her bed when she moved into Katie Ann's house.

Besides quilting, Jemima loves to play the organ. Last year, her church was getting rid of its organ and asked her if she would like it. "Why not?" was her response, and she and Katie Ann worked hard to clean it. In fact, now it is shined up and polished to such an extent that keeping one's foot on the pedal when playing is a challenge. Katie Ann has taken up the piano since her husband Ivan passed away not long ago, and her sister Emma took up the violin after she lost her husband at around the same time. The three women joke about taking their musical act on the road.

Jemima's greatest joy comes from spending time with her children, grandchildren, and great-grandchildren. She loves visitors, and has a guest book in her apartment which she unfailingly asks those who come to see her to sign.

Jemima reminisces occasionally about her childhood. She recalls a song she played on the piano when she was a young girl in school. It went: "I can read, I can write, I can smoke my daddy's pipe." She remembers the schoolhouse as having two stories, with first through fourth grade on the bottom level and the upper grades

on the top. She also remembers a time when, as a young mother, her son Eli became sick. She took him to the hospital by bus, and she recalls the doctors flushing out his system only to find her son incredibly bloated afterward. The eleven day stay in the hospital, including meals and treatment, cost $35.00- quite a bargain! She tried to remember how old her son was during his illness, but all she could remember was that he no longer wore a dress (both Amish girls and boys wear dresses until they are two years old).

Jemima continues quilting a bit longer, then admits she is tuckered out. She had gone into Mount Hope earlier that day and kept finding things she needed there, so she has accomplished quite a lot.

It is now time to rest a bit.

For many of the older residents of Holmes County, life is rich and full. They are as industrious as they can be for as long as they are able, and when they slow down, they are cared for by their extended family with the love and dignity they deserve. The work of Jemima Wengerd's life is evident in her family, in the care and respect they show towards her and towards each other. They live out the life lesson that the unflagging effort it takes to raise children and run a home is worthwhile. Jemima's legacy of devotion to her family has been gracefully and successfully passed down through three generations.

Above: Keeping a tradition.

Left: One must be diligent when navigating through fog and past slow-moving vehicles

Right: One never knows what will appear on the back of a buggy!

Above: Better clean those brakes.

Right: Can you find the girl giving her mother a loving hug?

Above: "Stellet euch nicht dieser Welt gleich."

Above: Faith in God